How to Draw Planes, Trains and Boats

Barbara Soloff Levy

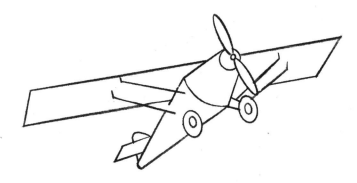

DOVER PUBLICATIONS, INC.
MINEOLA, NEW YORK

D0474318

Bibliographical Note

How to Draw Planes, Trains and Boats is a slightly altered republication of
the edition published by Dover Publications, Inc., in 2004. "Practice Pages"
have been added for this edition.

International Standard Book Number

ISBN-13: 978-0-486-47102-0
ISBN-10: 0-486-47102-0

Manufactured in the United States by Courier Corporation
47102004   2014
www.doverpublications.com

Note

Learning to draw planes, trains, and boats like the ones in this book is easier than it seems. If you follow the simple steps, you will discover how much fun it is to draw a jet fighter, a helicopter, a caboose, an antique locomotive, an ocean liner, and even a pirate ship!

Each page has four steps. Begin with the first step, and then add the second, third, and fourth steps to the drawing. It's a good idea to begin sketching using a pencil with an eraser, in case you change your mind about part of your picture. You may want to trace each step first to get a feel for drawing. Then try to draw on your own. Be sure to use the helpful Practice Pages, opposite the drawing pages. *Pay attention to the dotted lines—they should be erased when you have finished the last step of the drawing.*

When you are pleased with your drawing, you can go over the lines with a felt-tip pen or a colored pencil. Or you may choose to keep working at your drawing, erasing and then drawing in new lines until you are satisfied. After you complete your drawings, you can have even more fun by coloring them in.

With your new skills, you can begin to sketch the people and things around you. Use your imagination to create drawings of your own!

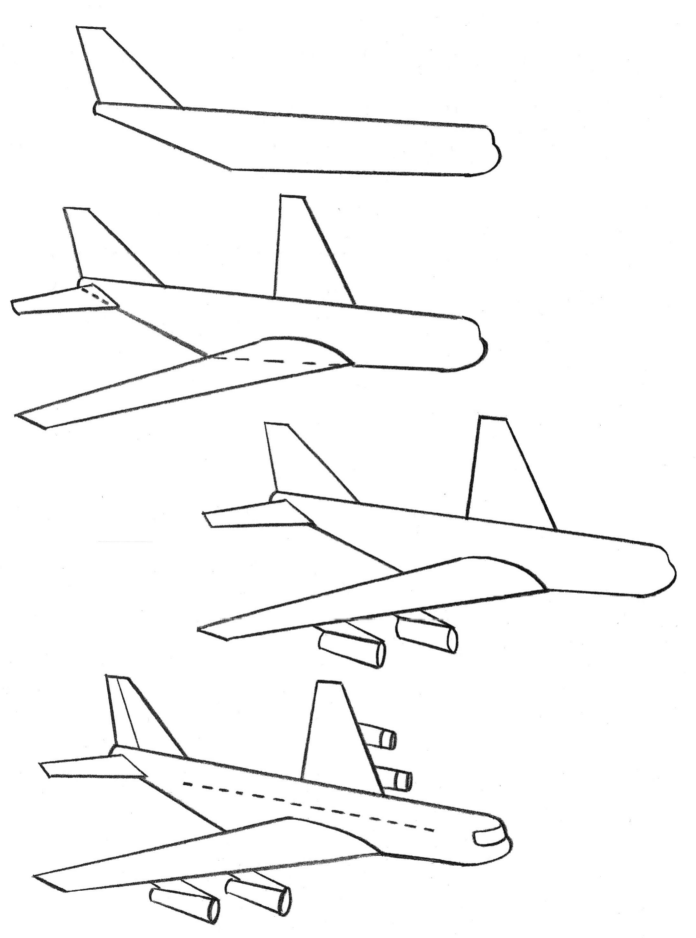

2   Passenger Jet

Practice Page

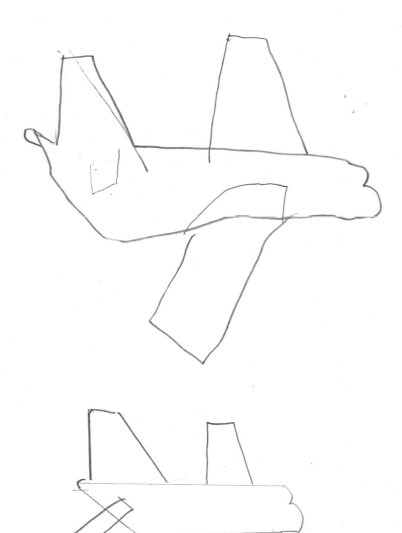

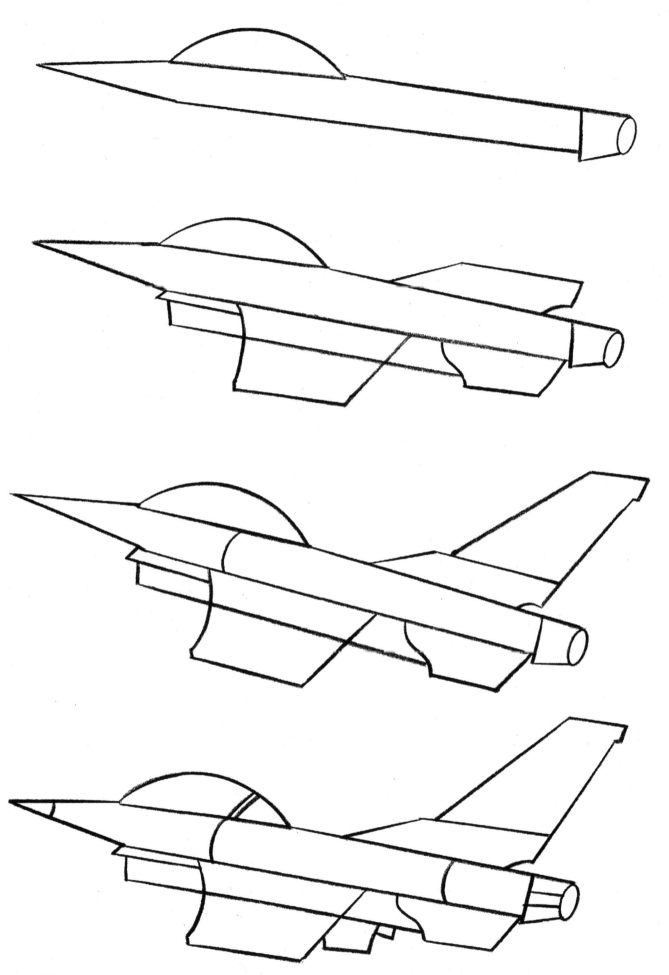

4   Jet Fighter

Practice Page

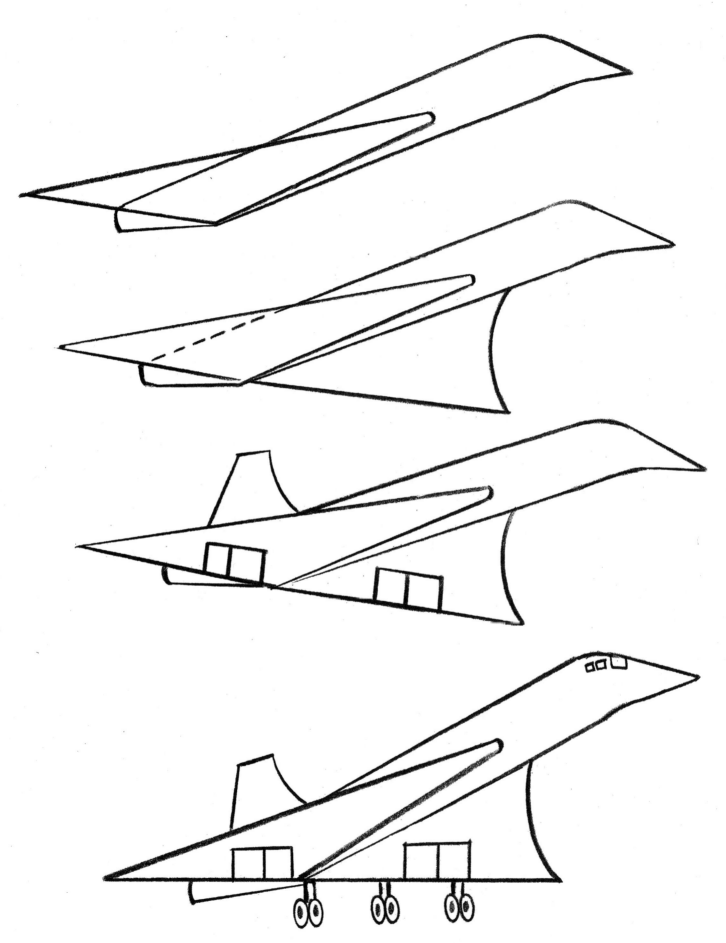

6　Concorde

Practice Page

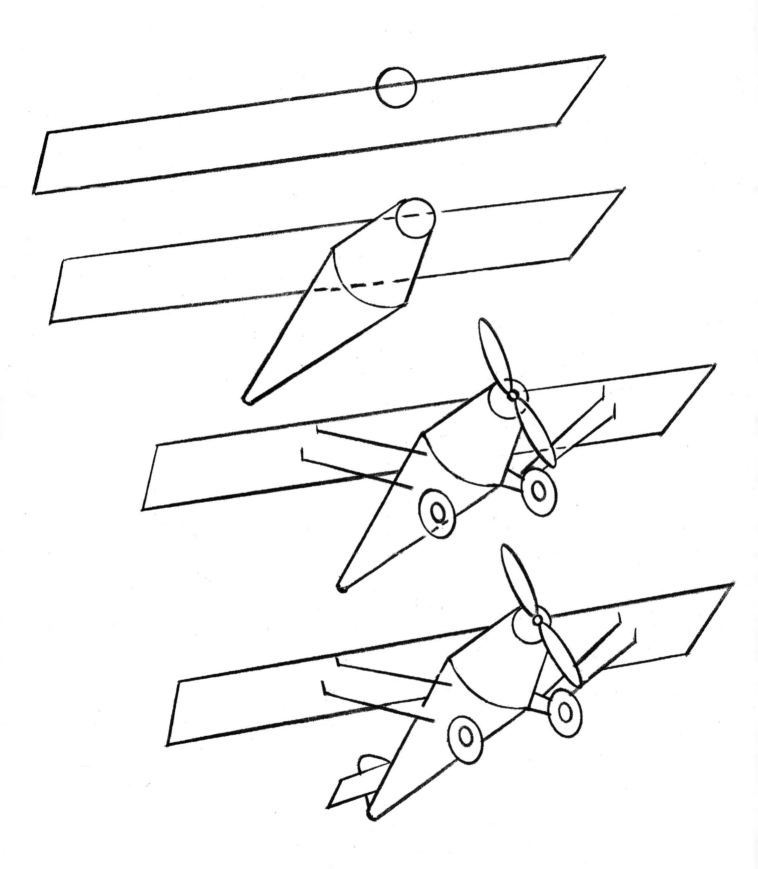

Practice Page

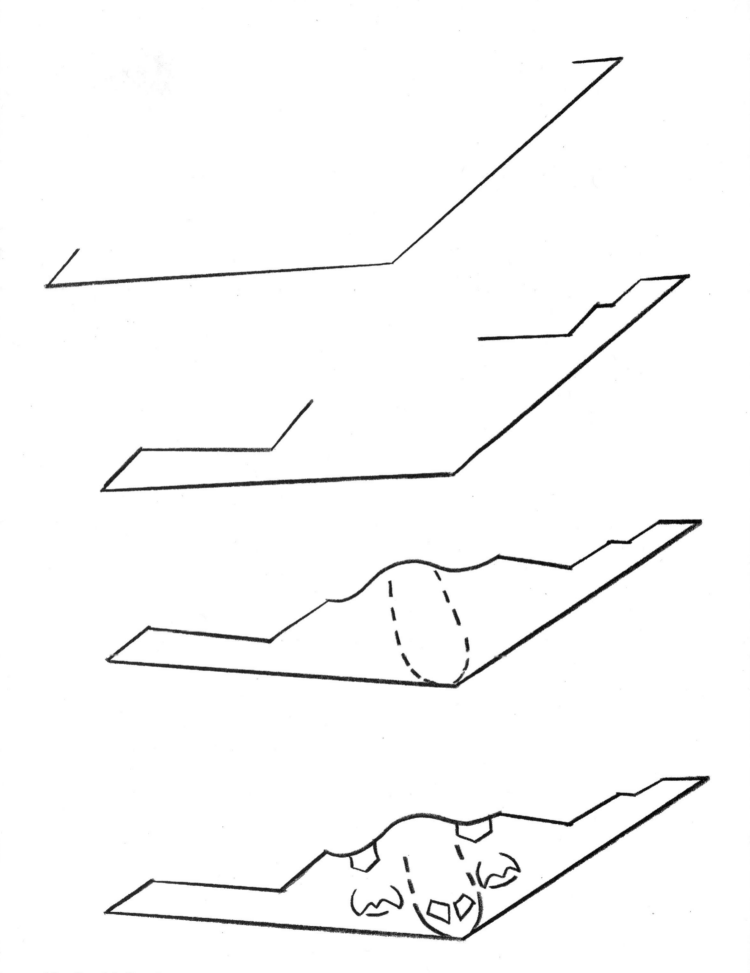

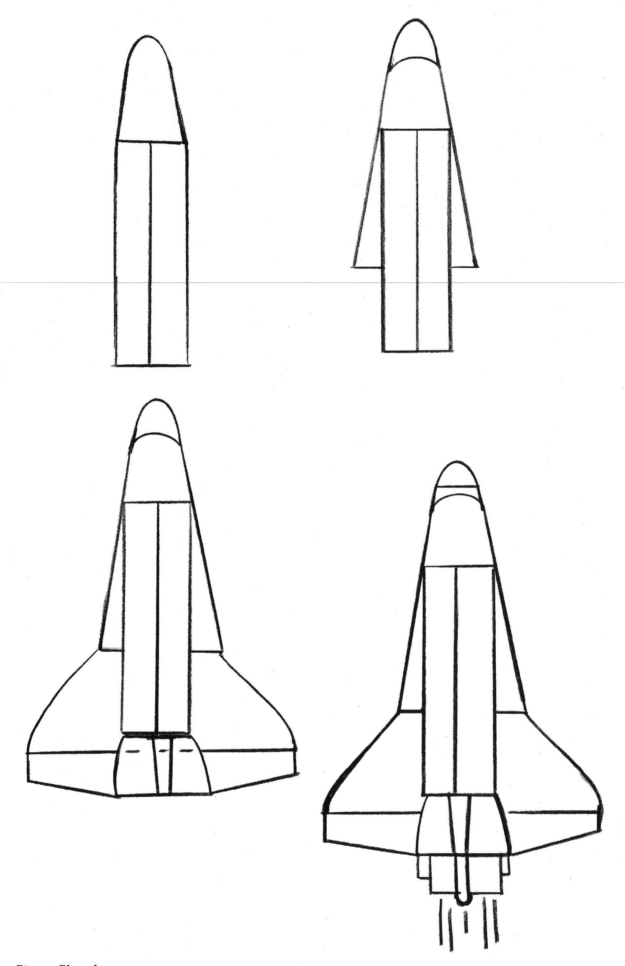

Practice Page

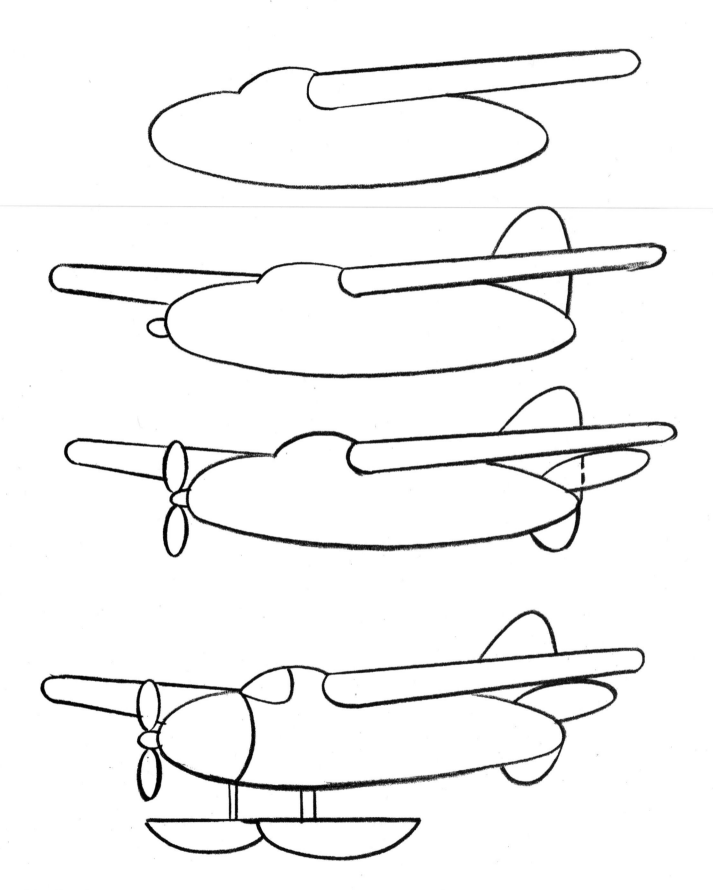

14 Seaplane

Practice Page

16 Piper Cub

Practice Page

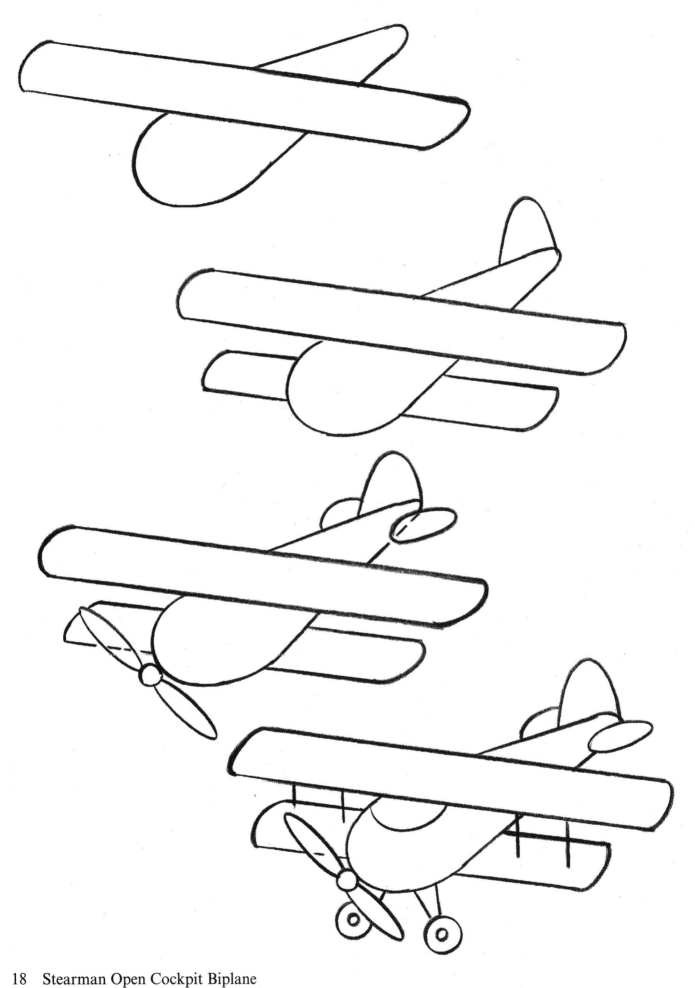

Practice Page

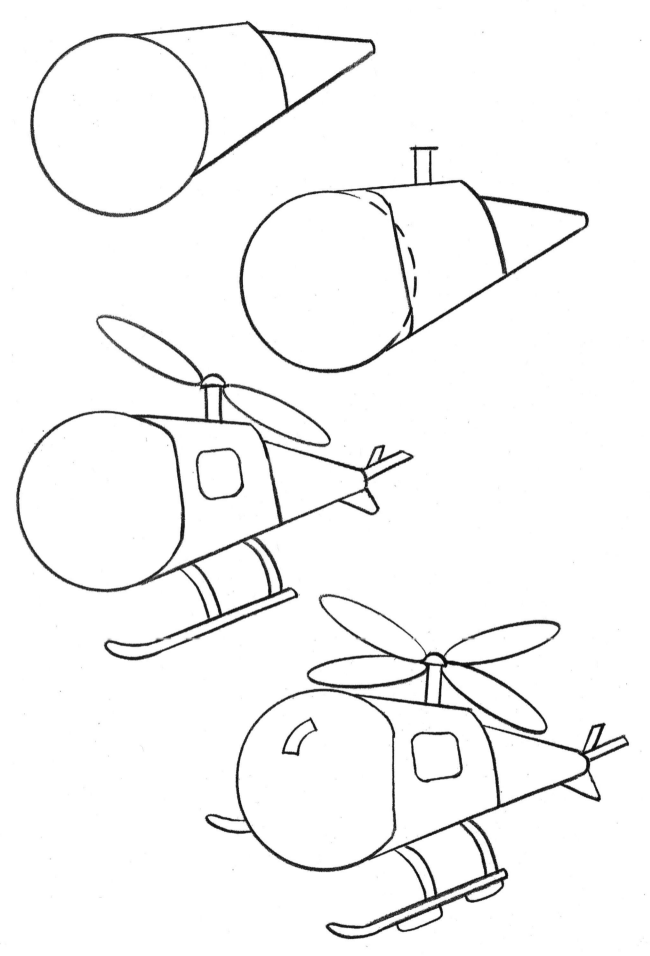

Practice Page

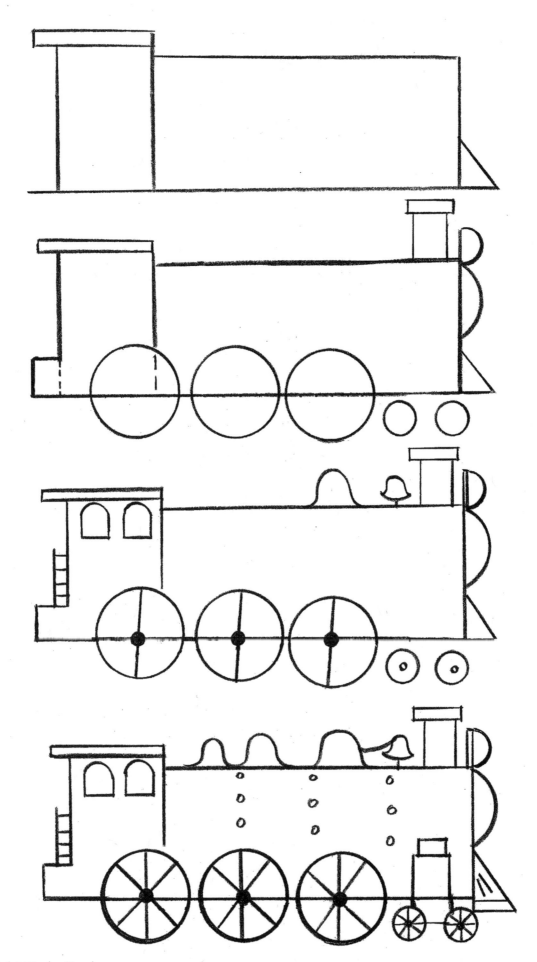

22   Freight Train Engine

Practice Page

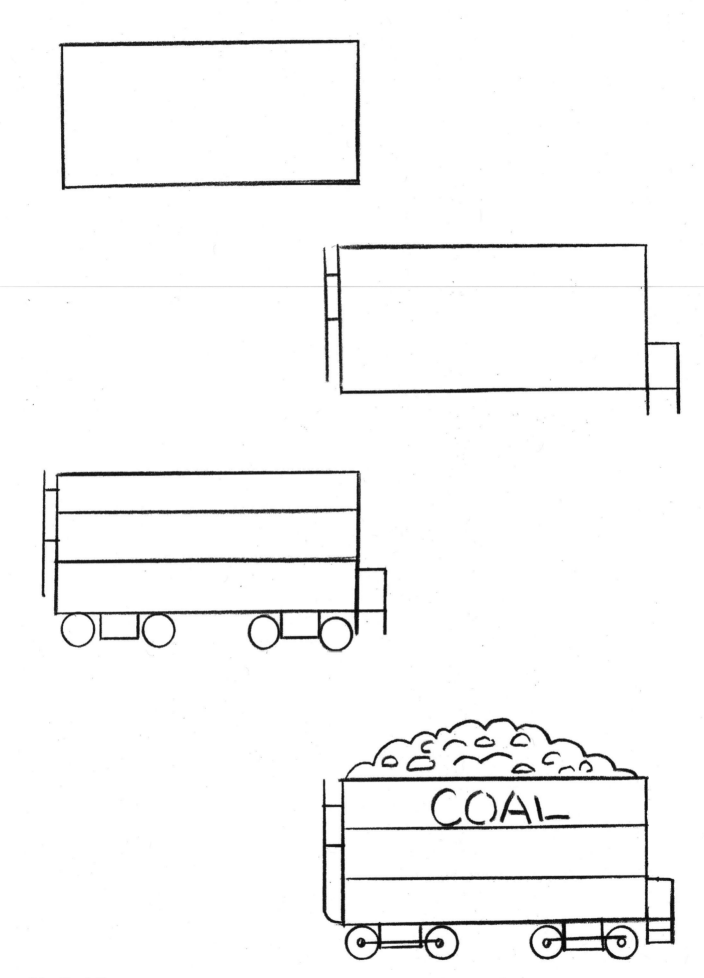

Practice Page

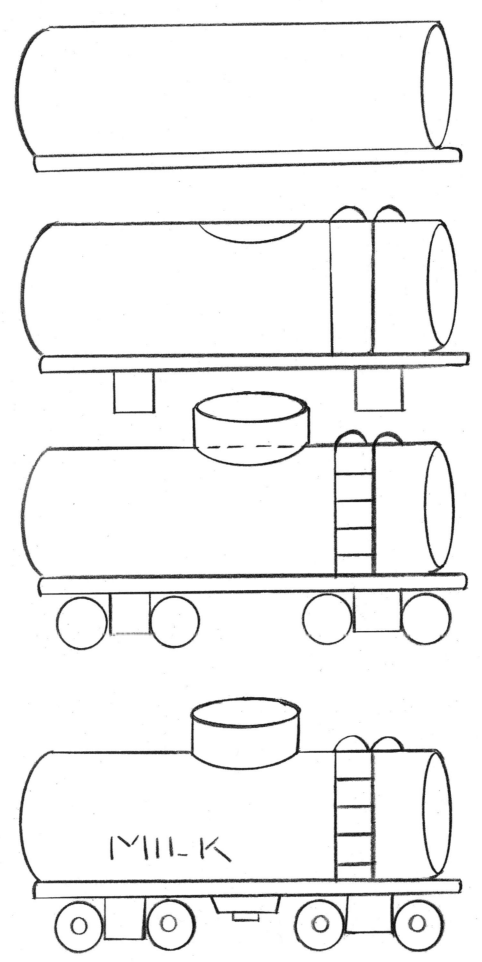

Practice Page

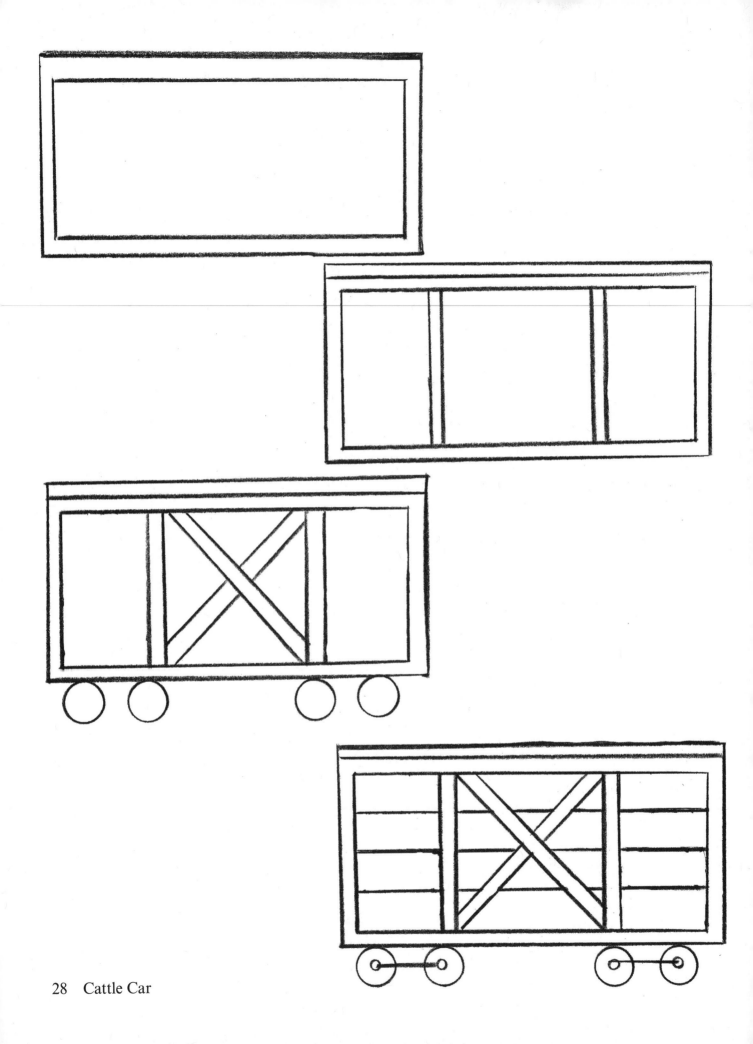

28   Cattle Car

Practice Page

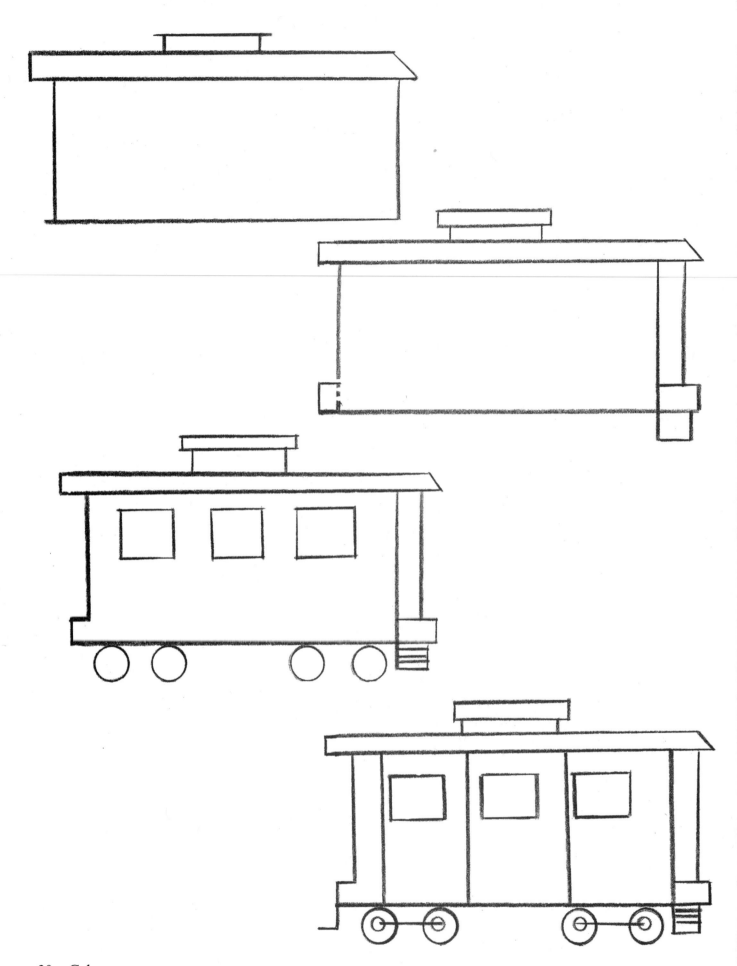

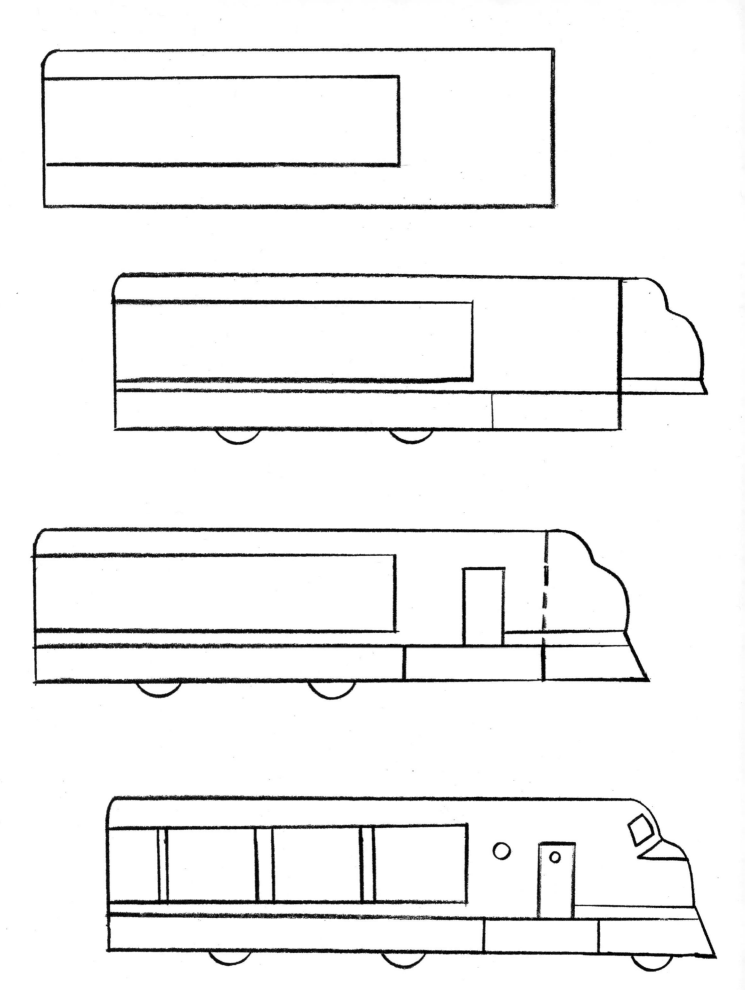

Practice Page

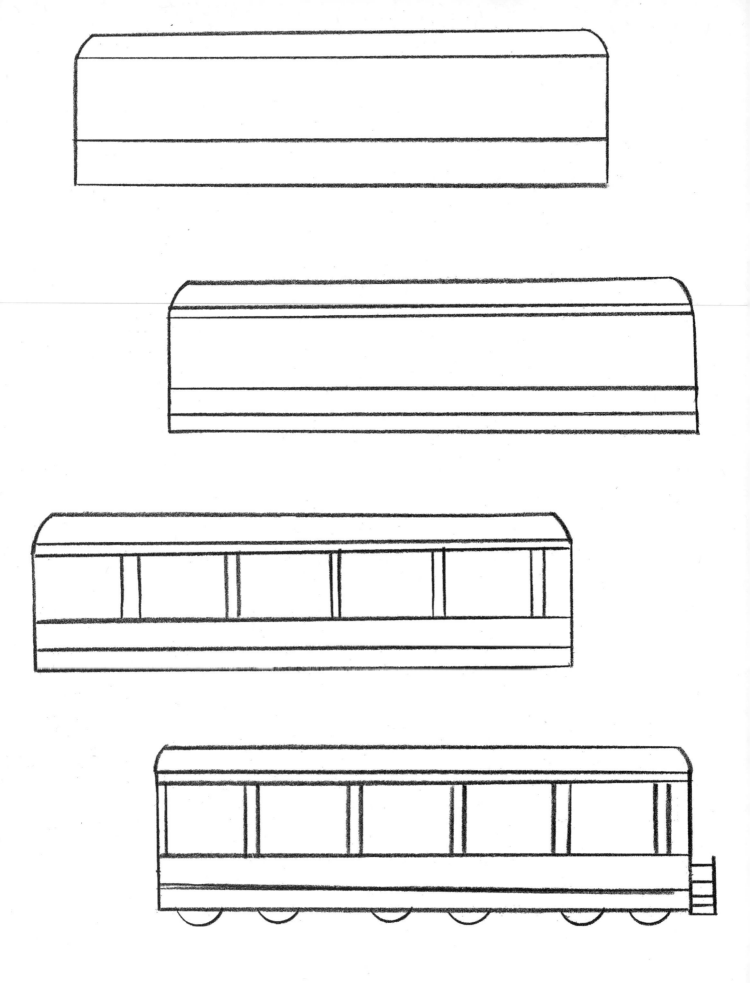

Practice Page

Practice Page

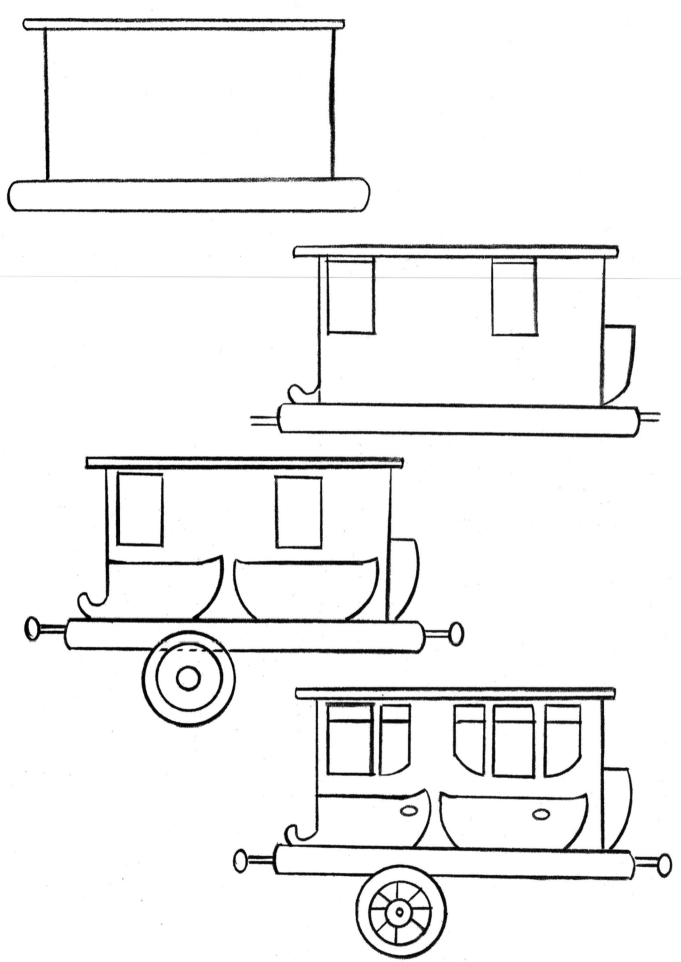

Practice Page

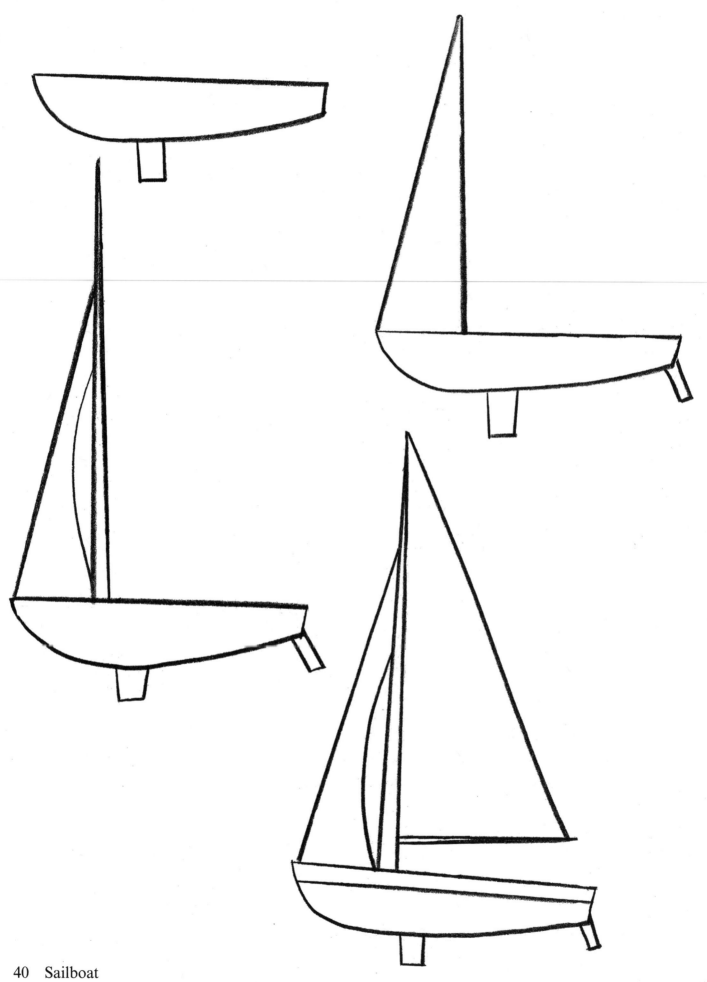

40   Sailboat

Practice Page

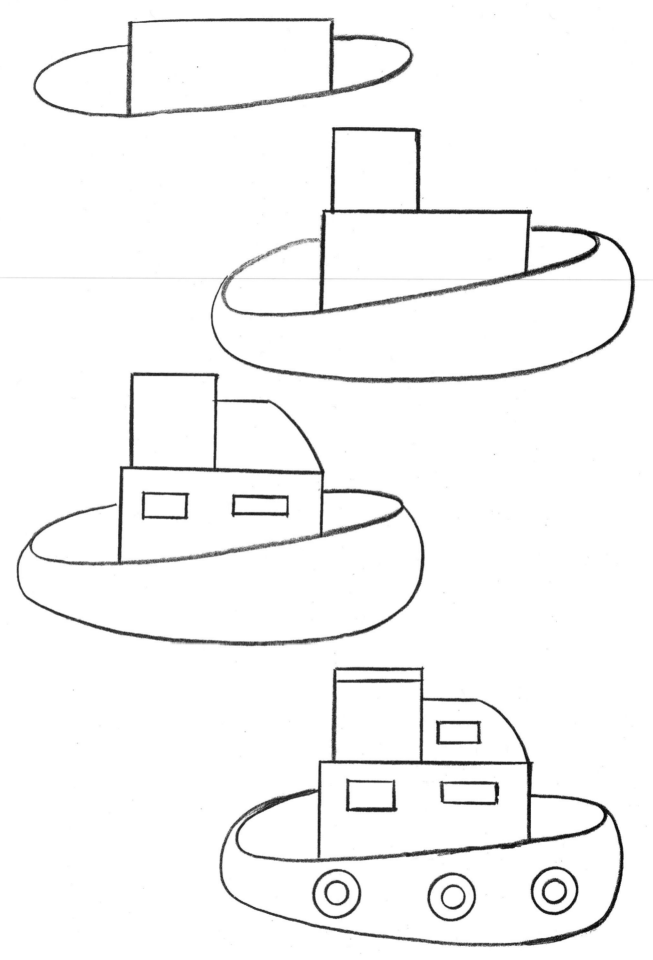

Practice Page

Practice Page

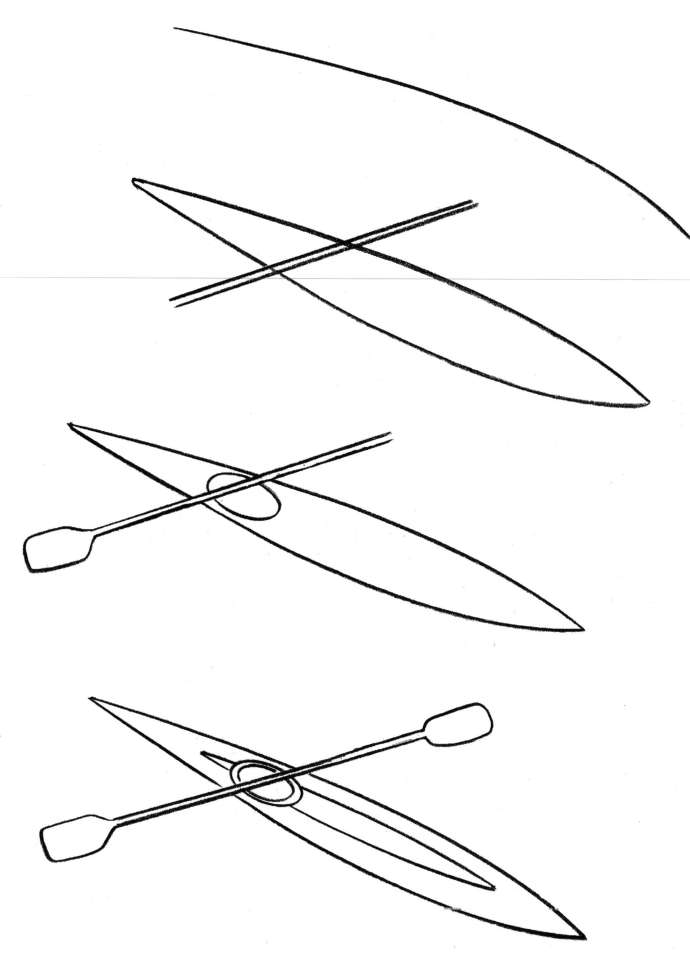

44 Kayak

Practice Page

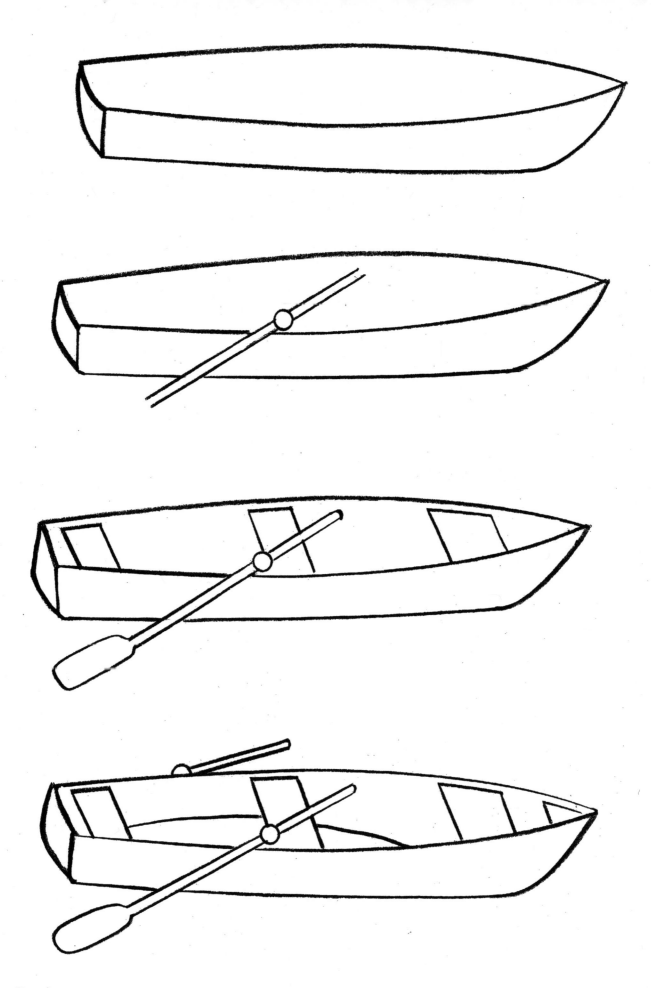

46 Rowboat

Practice Page

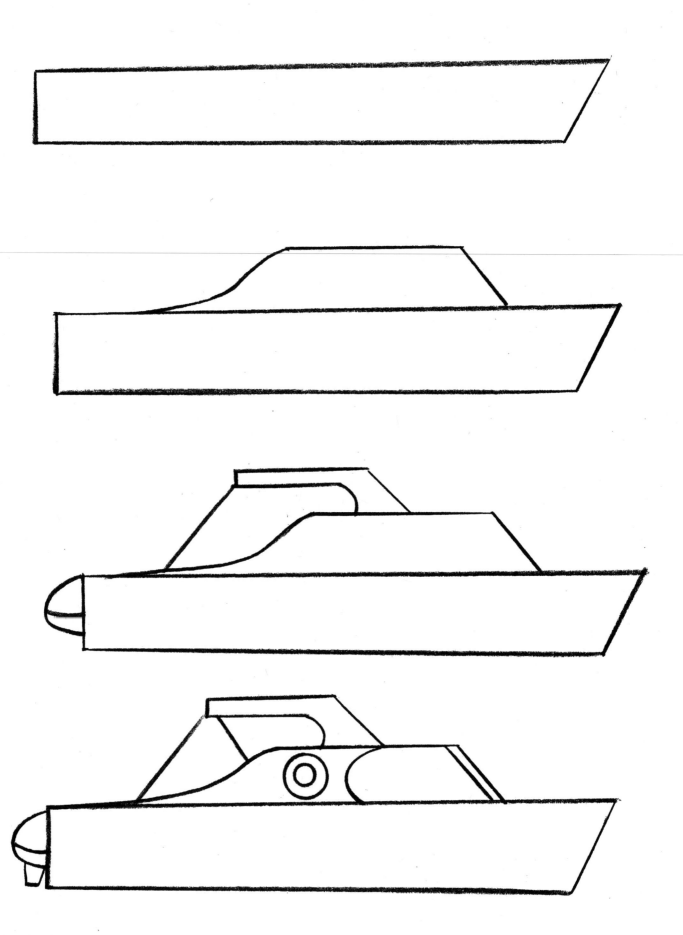

48   Cruiser

Practice Page

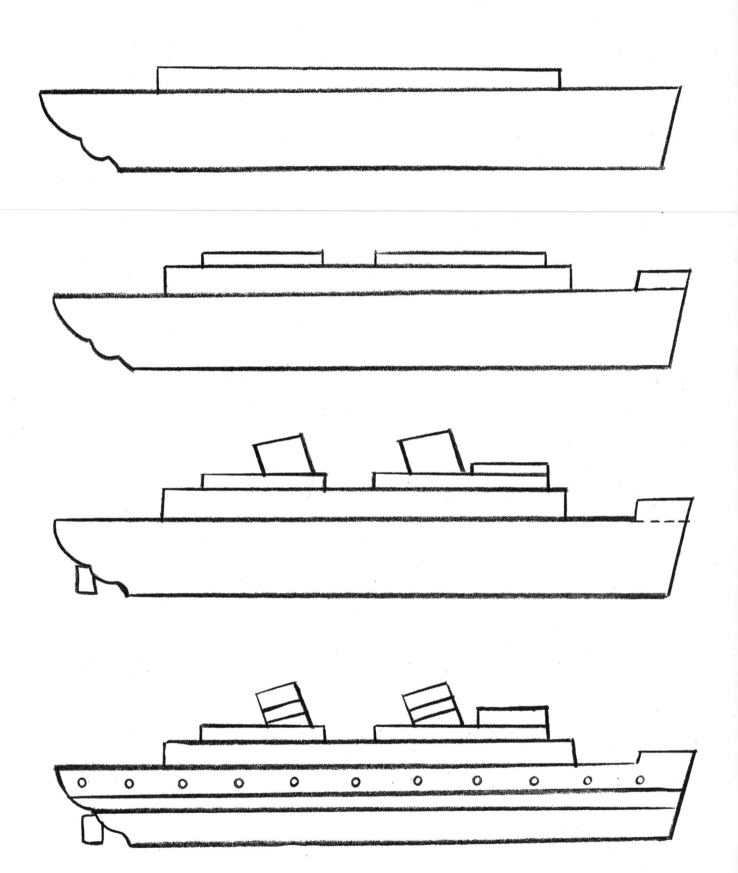

Practice Page

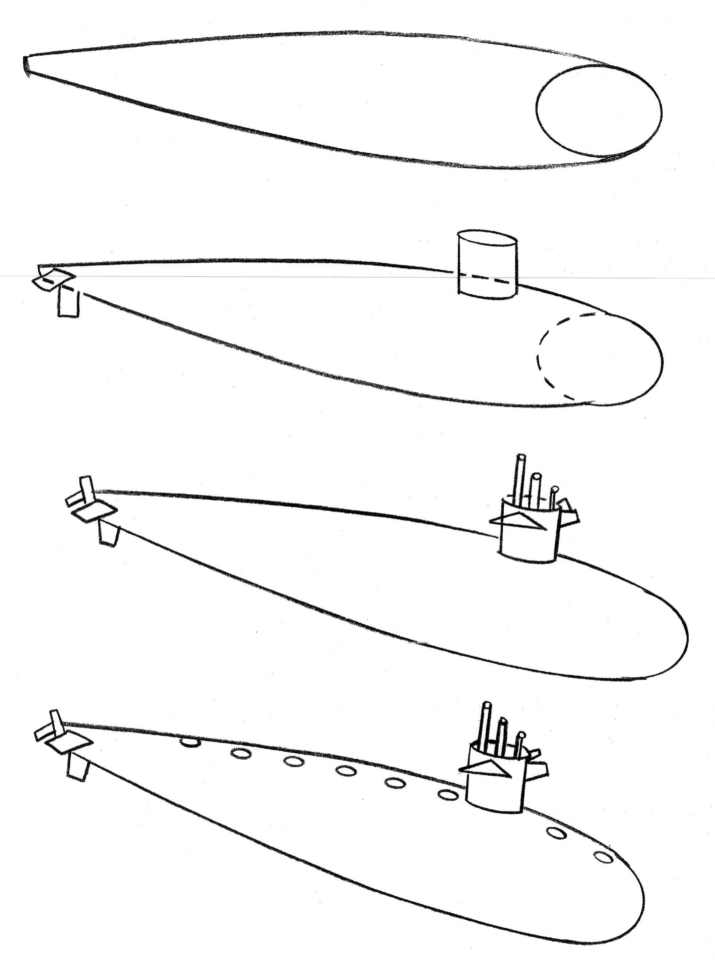

Practice Page

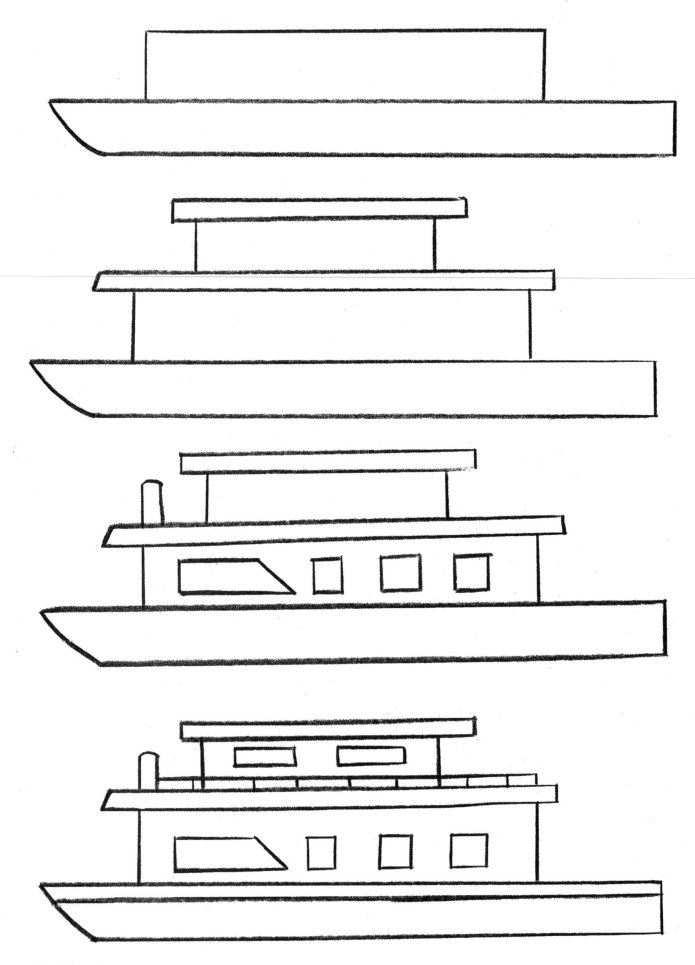

Practice Page

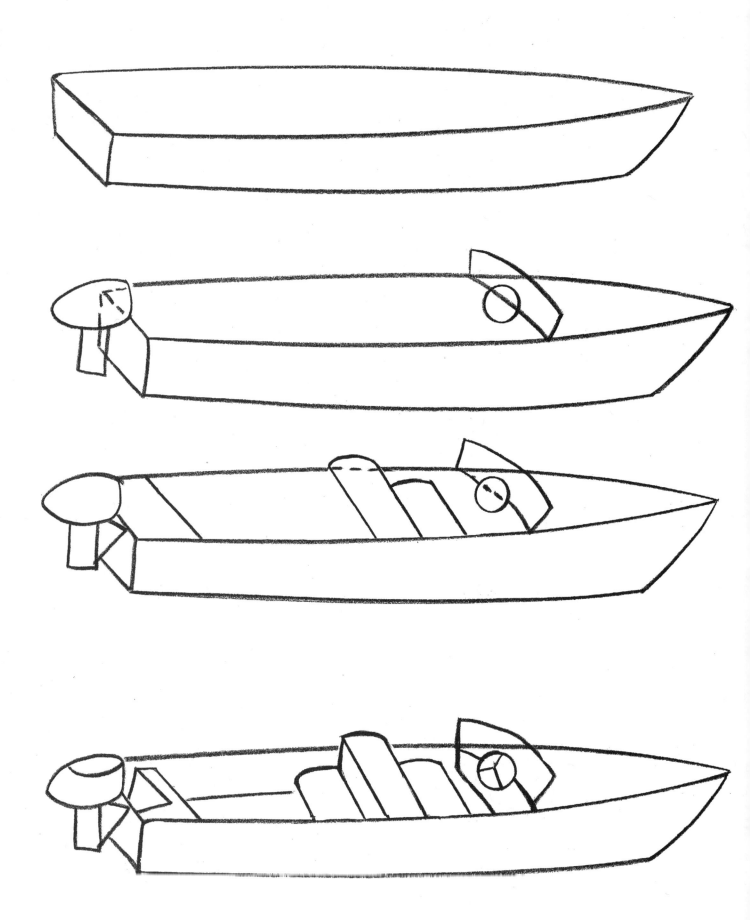

56 Speedboat

Practice Page

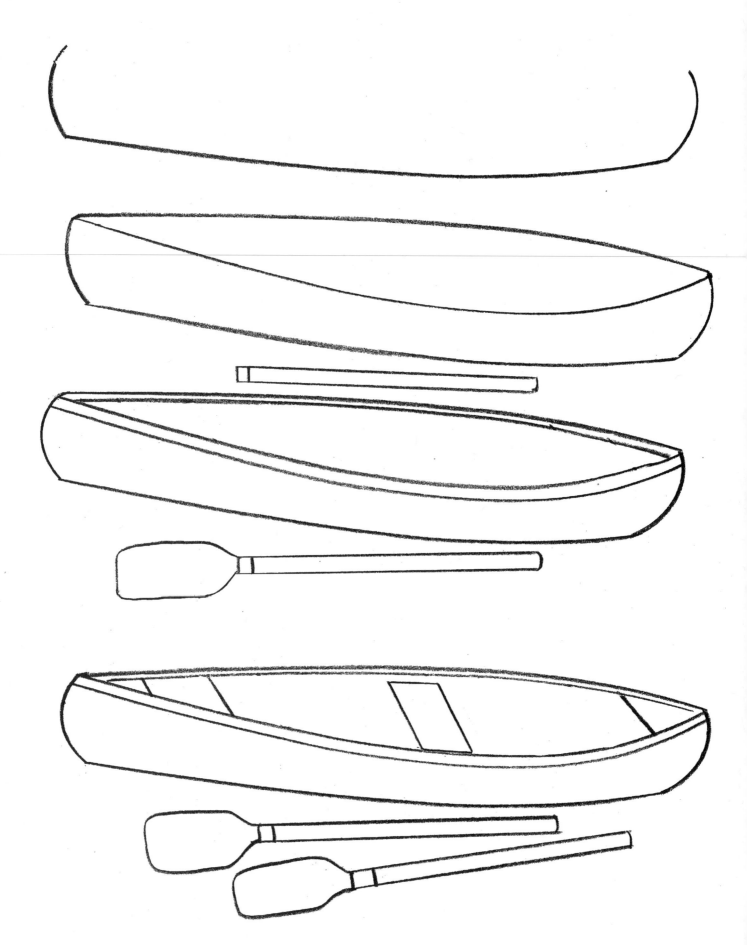

58 Canoe

Practice Page